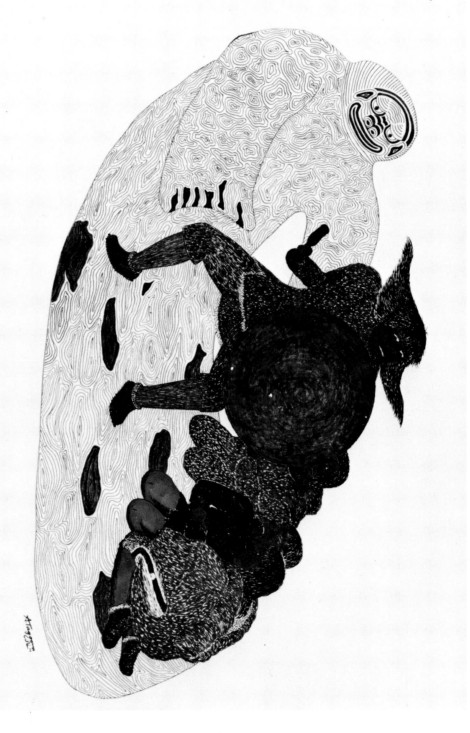

SHADOWS BY ARMAND TAGOONA A BOWS SHADOWS

Because Tagoona's Shadows is not so much a book as the experience—in images and words—of an unusual man revealed in ways not altogether close to ours, an introduction to it can be justified. An introduction not to the book, but to the experience. Not to Tagoona alone as an artist, but to Tagoona's being Inuit or inummarik, as he would say himself, meaning "real Inuk" or being really "total Eskimo." That is his life.

Shadows presents many facets of simultaneous coexistence: pure undividedness of reason and belief, of fact and fiction, biography and myth; the interchange of love and murder, of Christian faith and shamanistic power, of spirits hostile and benign. The opposites become united into life and energy as paradox of life, as affirmation of existence. That is Tagoona, that is the life of Shadows.

Perhaps Tagoona is more inummarik than most Inuit I know. I do not mean his physical appearance—his father, after all, was white, and he is delicately built, his face quite narrow with finely structured features; and he speaks English well, in fact, be it wrote this book in English, not in Inuktitut. Yet his thought—and his language, be it English or Inuktitu—is inummarik in structure, content, and in form. As is his life.

He and his family have moved from place to place in the Keewatin but have been back in Baker Lake since 1969. In many ways Tagoona and Baker Lake are now synonymous. Life there has shaped him into a new mould and he, in turn, has transformed life in Baker Lake. Not in accordance with his will but in response to revelations, through Bible reading, through Jesus' words—divinely, existentially—this is the way it was to be. . . .

He and indeed we too are instruments beyond our own manipulations once we have recognized that we must accept what we are asked to do in order to live fully. That was the way that faith, not religion, showed Tagoona: to follow God and not the institution. That was how he came to launch the Eskimo Christian Fellowship in Baker Lake, a strong communal core of mysticism and reality, of Inuitness heightened by religious relevance. Most of it bears Tagoona's imprint: un-self-consciously yet conscious—inummarik by profession of two faiths.

In these same years another transformation took place in Baker Lake: Sheila and Jack Butler came. The Butlers—husband and wife, both artists from Pittsburgh via Winnipeg—arrived in Baker Lake to help develop art and craft activities which, though supported by the government, had been neglected. The impact of the Butlers' dedication and their authority as artists sparked the community—art began to link life, past and present, with myth, tradition, craft and things inummarik. It was a happy fate that brought Tagoona and the Butlers together.

And John Robertson as well. John, a dealer and collector, was the first to recognize Tagoona's talents as an artist. He came to Baker Lake at just the right time to encourage the Butlers to convince Tagoona to do these drawings for a show in Ottawa. This was Tagoona's first exhibit, held at the Robertson Galleries in October 1972.

At that time there were only drawings with titles. Tagoona thought they were complete. We in the South, however, wanted and needed explanations. And though Tagoona "never planned to write" and said, "it was very difficult to translate all my drawings," he did agree to put into words the thoughts behind the drawings. The Butlers helped him to express himself in English, yet to retain his inummarik thoughts and images.

Because Tagoona's writing was as vivid as his drawing, Alma Houston, friend of many artists in the North, saw at once that words and images together would make "a fine book." And so they did, because they were all one, like an inummarik cycle of experience.

Reality is grasped in words and visions, as myths and metaphors play an important part in everyday living. The self becomes part of history—autobiography is extracted from the myths and legends and becomes projected into, and renewed in, myths.

Tagoona's drawings are fusions of thought and images, of memory and dreams, of past and present. The past is brought forward. It is made real through imagery. The logic of the image is its power to convince, its faculty to speak without the use of words. Words have other uses. Tagoona's drawings are drawn metaphors. Thus in this book there are two mixes doubly intertwined: the mix of myth and life, of past and present on one hand; the mix of word and image, of thought and vision, on the other.

We in the South—believing in the processes of reason and analysis—tend to divide, to take apart, to fragment. We understand the parts but often fail to see the whole. Or we expect the whole to be the sum of all its parts. The whole is

—and contains—much more than all its parts. The whole may also be not one, but many: simultaneous opposites, a range of meanings and of values, co-existing to underline life's mystery, irrationality, profoundness, incomprehensibility, grandeur, cruelty, capriciousness, complexity, perfection, rawness and simplicity.

Tagoona's special quality is a sense of wonder, accepting and affirming all that is life and all that lies beyond one's comprehension and endurance. Through myth and art he reaffirms this sense of wonder and pulls together parts, reunites fragments, heals the separated and builds a whole.

George Swinton
Carleton University, 1975

PLATE I

Not so very long ago I was told by someone who saw my drawings that when I was still very small I used to draw images of human beings that were as real as living ones. I suppose there is some truth in it.

On the other hand, I was told by someone else that my drawings are too real, that anybody can draw like that. I was tempted then to draw something that is not real to me, something I have never seen. But to me this is like drawing a lie just to make people interested in my drawings and to get a high price for them. I have seen some drawings in the Craft Shop that have no real source, no history at all, created by the artist himself from nothing, because there is a rumour that that's the kind of thing *qablunaat*, or white people, like. Every time a white person saw a horror figure drawn by an Eskimo, he was fascinated by it, because maybe he believed that Eskimos think that way. I know that in the case of some horror drawings, the artist got the idea first from comic books. We also know that a person cannot help himself from copying other people's ideas. Oh yes, he changes it a little to make it look like his own and no-one else's. I do that sometimes. I don't think this is very wrong; I think it is worse to draw something I have never seen or heard of myself.

I will go back now in my mind and try to remember my beginnings as an artist. Although I do not think of myself as an artist. I remember one of the first pictures that fascinated me when I was about five or six years old. We lived near Igloolik. The picture I saw was on a can of pipe tobacco, which my father bought from the Hudson's Bay Company

in Repulse Bay. On that can there was a big bird, an eagle? That picture used to get hold of me and I would look at it for a long time, until the bird became alive. Then, "Where's my pipe tobacco?" my father wondered. "Here," I said. There were also a few other things from the Hudson's Bay Company that had pictures on them that used to fascinate me.

At that time my father had a rifle and bullets. I used to use a bullet as a pencil. The point of a bullet is lead, and that lead made good marks. I drew many things with it, human beings and animals and birds. Even adults used to use bullets for pencils when they were writing to each other.

Some time later we moved into the settlement at Repulse Bay, where the Hudson's Bay Company and Revillon Frères, both traders, used to compete, trying to get the most furs from the Eskimos. There was also a Roman Catholic mission there, surprisingly. I was a member of that church with its two big, strong, black-robed and long-black-bearded priests. In their house and in the church there were many things that captivated me, pictures and drawings of heavenly people. Or at least that is what I thought they were. There were also pictures of fire, in that place *tuungraaluk* where the great evil one is king. He lived in the fire yet he did not burn or catch fire. But his poor people were suffering as they dropped down into the fire. These pictures became alive before my eyes. When I looked away they stayed in my mind for a long time after. In fact they are still in my mind after some 40 years.

The pencil and I have been working together very closely

PLATE 2

I used to look at my mother's face that way. When someone is smoking tobacco, the smoke goes down instead of going up. Why don't you see it for yourself?

I was born in 1926 in Repulse Bay, NWT, of mixed blood, Eskimo blood from my mother and German blood from the man. My real name is Tagungrnaaq. My mother named me after her mother. In *Inuktut*, Eskimo way, there is no difference between men's and women's names. When my mind opened to see and understand and decide things on my own, I became very religious. I was a member of the Roman Catholic church in Repulse Bay. Oh yes, I did a few things against religion while I was still a boy, seven or eight years old. I stole some things that tasted good to my mouth, and let my nose touch a girl's nose. Some people say that Eskimos kiss like dogs, rubbing their noses.

Later my parents and I moved to Chesterfield Inlet, NWT, where I became Anglican, and after that we moved to Baker Lake. And I became a stronger Anglican than ever, still very religious. Here in Baker Lake, my first job was with the RCMP, when I was fifteen. My mother died in 1944 while having a baby in Chesterfield Inlet Roman Catholic Hospital. Maybe I should mention here that I am the only one who lived among my brothers and sisters. They all died, about ten of them, before birth or soon after. Am I living because of my German blood? Well, I didn't like Germans in the 1940s. We heard in those years that there was a big, big fight started by Hitler, the German boss. We heard that he was a very bad man. He's dead now, a long time ago, I guess.

for years now. I learned that if you don't put your thoughts onto paper with marks and see them with your eyes, they will get lost from your mind. I have learned too, that your mind and your hands work very differently. Your mind can do anything but your hands cannot. I could be a real artist in my mind, but my hands cannot do the work. When I wanted to draw a picture, I thought of something first, then I would try to draw it. But the idea never comes out exactly the way I wanted it. I think this was my hands' mistake.

My drawings are not, any of them, exactly the way I wanted them to be. I am not really satisfied with even one drawing I have done. Some of my drawings are completely from my own ideas, and so there is no story behind them; I mean no traditional or true story. I have to invent the story if I am to talk about those drawings. Some are from the old stories that were carried from the past through the minds of Eskimos, and we know these stories have been changed a lot because they are not written down. But there must be a true story behind each of these. The storyteller would change it a little because he would forget a few things here and there, and the next man would change it again, and what do we get after 50 storytellers, every one of them changing the story a little from the first? That is why, I am sure, some drawings of old legends are so strange.

Sometimes too, I am tempted to draw strange living beings in strange places. By the way, did you ever look at the face of a person upside down? It's funny. If you want to try it, just get your own head upside down and look into another's face, while he is eating or smiling or talking. It's very funny.

PLATE 3

comes from individuals, Eskimos and whites, for our work here in Baker Lake, and not from the church. We are Christians, we believe the Bible and try our best to live and work by it.

These are a few of the things I have done in my life. My wife and I have eleven children living, from nine to 30 years old, seven boys and four girls, two babies died; thirteen children born from my wife.

I am often asked how the Inuit felt about being brought into settlements. It is not an easy thing to talk about; the Inuk himself is not sure how he feels. I myself have lived in settlements nearly all my life but I tasted a little "out there" in the Inuit camps in winter. I love it "out there."

In the past, even in the early part of my lifetime, when there was a camp where three to five families lived, they usually put their tents quite a distance apart from each other. In the winter too, they built their iglus, or snow houses, quite a distance from each other, something like one or two hundred yards. You wonder why so far, why not right next door? Because they say they don't want to make trouble for another family, caused by their children or themselves. There are no two who think the same or decide in the same way. What about now? There are from 200 to 1000 Inuit living together in one settlement. Do they get along smoothly and nicely? Gymnasiums and community halls are built so the Inuit can play games. Is this intended to make us more friendly to each other? I wonder. I think sometimes more jealousy comes out of these things. Oh well, it can't be helped now, because the new Inuit of today are

A few months after my mother's death I got fired from my job because of a little argument between the police and myself. "You're fired. Don't ever come back here," he said. I never did. After that, for three years I was just a hunter, killing anything that moved when I could, except human beings of course.

Those were three years of good life and fun. Oh yes, by that time I was a married man. I married a wonderful girl, also of mixed blood, Eskimo blood from her mother and white man's blood from the man. We were married in 1944 in August, a year before my mother died. After three years of that good and happy life I started to work with the RCAF in Baker Lake, driving tractors and helping with the fixing of broken parts. And then in 1952 I was offered a job with the Department of Transport Radiosonde station in Baker Lake. That job lasted until 1958. In that year I moved with my family to Rankin Inlet, NWT to be a missionary among the miners, both white people and Eskimos. In 1959 I was ordained as a deacon in the Anglican church in Rankin Inlet. In 1960 I was ordained to the priesthood in Toronto. A bishop next? I wondered about that. But I have made up my mind that I would refuse to become a bishop. To me a bishop should be an old man. From Rankin Inlet we were sent to Eskimo Point to do missionary work there.

In 1969 we moved back to our old home in Baker Lake. Home sweet home? Many things had been changed, many ways of doing things. The Bishop did not send me back; we just moved on our own. In 1971 I resigned from the Anglican priesthood, but I am still a missionary. Our support

PLATE 4

players of games and do not face the serious life that the early Inuit used to.

Before I talk more about today's life, let me go back to about 30 years ago. I was here in the Baker Lake settlement. It was still very small. There were only the Hudson's Bay Company, the RCMP, the Roman Catholic mission and the Anglican mission. At that time there were only about 22 Inuit, children and all, and six *qablunaat* or white people, no white women. The police laws were very strict about hunting caribou in the spring—June and July. In those two months caribou usually came near the Baker Lake settlement in thousands, driven to the shore by mosquitoes. I remember well one time, in the year 1952, in early July, thousands of caribou came to the shore as usual, just across the lake. So every man went off across the lake with his canoe. It was not easy because there was still lots of ice in front of the settlement, but we managed to cross the ice, walking and pulling the canoe along. When we hit water we started the motor. Off we went! But we didn't know that just behind us, about half a mile away, the police were trying to catch us to stop us from going after the caribou because it was out of season. My father and I and another canoe with two men were in front and all the rest were way behind. So our two canoes reached the caribou and we wondered where the others were because they never came. After that hunt we found out that they were caught by the police and stopped from going any farther. The police took all their rifles away from them and told them to go back, which they did. The police were still trying to catch our two canoes but failed, because they didn't have enough gas in their gas tank. So the police decided to go back. We four men didn't know what went on behind us. We killed enough caribou and carried them to our boats and went back to the settlement. One of the men who was turned back by the police came to us and told us what had happened. He also told us that the police were waiting for us. My heart jumped a little; I was scared, but I tried to act as if I were not. We reached home in the middle of the night because we didn't want the police to see us with all that meat in our canoes. The next day the policeman and his Inuk helper came to me. The policeman said, "I want your rifle."

"Oh!" I said.

"I want your rifle," he said again, this time a little louder.

I said, "Why?"

He said, "That's my duty, because you hunt when hunting season is closed."

I said, "Come, I'll give you my rifle but please don't let it get rusty."

Then he said, "Don't worry, it will be cleaner than it is now when you get it back, when the hunting season is open. That will be the middle of September."

"Okay," I said, "I have another rifle, you want that too?"

He said, "No." I said to myself, "I will go again after the caribou before September with my other rifle." With that in my mind the police and I parted. He had my one rifle and walked away with it to his office. All the rest of the hunters' rifles were kept in the police office until the season was open. When the season opened, our rifles were given back to us,

PLATE 5

all shiny, cleaned and polished. But before this, all the hunters hunted caribou because all of us had other rifles at home. But we thanked the police for cleaning and polishing the rifles they took from us. And too, we and the other men who were not caught by the police had lots of caribou meat because they didn't take the meat away from us.

Let me go back again about 30 years, and go to the land, inland where no white man lived. I never lived with them there in the summer but I know how they lived and worked and rested. Inland, there is a time to work and a time to be lazy. In the middle of the summer, about mid-August, a man was busy. Every morning, if possible, if bad weather didn't stop him, he got up and ate his morning food, whatever he had. He took his telescope, rifle and a piece of rope about six to ten feet long, which he would use to carry a caribou if he shot one. He also took his pocket knife and tobacco, of course, and his pipe and went off to the closest high hill. From that place he searched the land all around through the telescope, very carefully, for an hour or even two long hours from the same spot. From that hill he looked all around an area of about fifteen to twenty miles. If the high hill was very high he could see for many more miles around. He didn't have to walk all these miles when he had the telescope. Why walk when you don't have to? If he didn't see any caribou, and if he had some meat at home, he went back to his tent. He may even have slept a little because he needed it. He was preparing himself for the work ahead, because he knew that soon there had to be caribou, and he would have to kill and skin and cache as many as he could. That is

hard work, especially caching the skinned caribou by piling rocks around and on top of them.

After a little sleep he got up again and went off to the same high hill, and looked around again through the telescope. If again he did not see caribou he might go home and sleep a little more or he might go farther to another high hill and look from there. So he went from hill to hill and by doing that he covered many miles through the telescope —the telescope he bought from the Hudson's Bay Company recently, or maybe years ago. When he saw a caribou he went off toward it. He approached it very slowly and carefully. When the caribou was very close, he fired and the animal was dead without ever seeing the man. If there was more than one caribou, five or ten, a man usually killed them all if he was careful, because he knew which caribou to kill first, second, third and so on. He also watched the movement of the animals when they noticed the noise of the rifle and the killing. When the man killed ten caribou there was lots of work. He had to skin and carry them, one by one, to a spot or to several places where there were loose rocks. With the rocks he covered them all, all around, so foxes and wolves couldn't get at them during the fall and winter. This was a man's work on the land from about the middle of August to early November; killing caribou, as many as he could, for the long winter.

What about another man in another inland camp who found himself where there were no caribou? If there was not even one caribou to be seen for two months. August and September, what would you do? Your wife and five children!

PLATE 6

If you got nothing at all, you couldn't leave them behind if you decided to walk a hundred or three hundred miles to the settlement where the Hudson's Bay Company store was, and the police station. Why did I mention police? It may sound strange to you if I say the RCMP used to give out food to the starving, but that is true. They used to. And the Hudson's Bay Company too. I have heard Inuit saying today that you can never get anything free from the Hudson's Bay Company. But they can, if they have to. And we Inuit thank them very much indeed when we remember the past, when there was no government around. And to the police too we are thankful. Police are not living there only to put you in jail or to stop you from doing bad deeds. They used to be one of our hopes against starvation. Nowadays some white people tell us we don't need police in the North; even some Inuit say that. How forgetful we are, like a son who, when he is able to support himself, forgets his father's support when he was small or in need.

A man who found himself where there were no caribou would kill small animals, ptarmigan and any other birds that could be eaten, and he would fish too if he was to survive until caribou came within his reach. In the middle of October in some years the lakes were covered with ice. When this happened a family had more hope of surviving —they could fish through the ice. By that time the starving family might come to know of a camp that was not too far from where they were. They would take down their tent, and taking everything they needed, they would move on toward the other camp. By doing this they survived starva-

tion. Those who had meat shared it with others.

Long winter came for all Inuit in the North. In November, iglus, or snow houses; small iglus for small families, big iglus for large families. Each family built its own. No-one built it for them unless a man was very weak for some reason. Long winter—November, December, January, February, March, April, May. By June it's getting warm, July is too hot and the time for mosquitoes, but there are lots of caribou then. In the long winter lots of things happened and lots of things didn't happen. There was time to work and time to be lazy. When the fair weather came a man went out from the iglu and set his fox traps and went off to check them every week if possible. When a snowstorm came, the family just stayed inside the iglu waiting for the end of it. This was not a hard life if a family had supplies of meat for the whole winter. But if there was no meat supply this could be hard and tragic, because fair weather or stormy they would have to go out and fish through the hole they dug in the ice. It was their only hope of survival.

The well-to-do families would trap foxes. I remember some men used to trap 200 foxes in two or three months, some only ten or so. Then they travelled by dog team to the settlement of Baker Lake to trade their foxes to the Hudson's Bay Company. Most Inuit did this during the season before December so they could go back home with the food and materials they brought from the Bay to their wives and children, and then trap again for a few weeks before they came to the settlement for the Christmas feast. Some brought their whole families to the settlement for the Christ-

PLATE 7

mas season, but only a few. Those who came for Christmas usually arrived on the 23rd, some on the 24th, even some on the 25th. After the Christmas season Inuit traded their foxes. After this, all the inland Inuit went off to their homes. At home they trapped foxes until the season was closed; in some years April 15, in others at the end of April.

So the Inuit went on living; that was the main thing—to live on. Nobody really thought of the death that was coming to each one of them. As much as I can remember, the danger of starvation usually came in early spring, or just before, in April and May.

Every year spring came to all Inuit in June and July. June was the best time, if there were caribou and fish around their camp. And best of all, the geese were back again in the North from the South. That was the lazy time again, to eat whenever they wanted, and sleep whenever they wanted to and as long as they wanted.

What I have written about so far is the life of the inland Inuit in the past. Now what happened to those of us who lived in Baker Lake all year round when schools and government people started to move in. Before all this I remember the most important thing was when DC-3 airplanes started to come to Baker Lake, in the year 1946. It was early spring when they landed on the Baker Lake ice, just in front of the settlement. Before that, two big tractors pulling behind them a cabin and fuel drums arrived here from Churchill in wintertime. To us it was a time of wonder and amazement. The next day these two big machines pushed up a pile of snow on the lake, to make a long runway for the

airplanes that were to land on it in the following few days. Yes, then airplanes came and went from Churchill, bringing in drums of gas, two or three times a day. We were wondering what was going on, then we heard rumours that war, the big fight, might be started any time by the Russians. It was an exciting time for us all and we were a little scared at the same time. And we didn't feel like hunting any more for some reason. We just wanted to watch all the airplanes landing and taking off. Then in spring lots of army men came to Baker Lake and put up their tents where the land air strip is now. They made a lot of noise, day and night, with the two big machines that came from Churchill during the winter. And they scraped the land slowly. When we got near their tents, we heard them talking and laughing. So we never got inside their tents, because they were like animals, jumping up and down, laughing and shouting, and jumping and swimming in the lake where we got our drinking water, and they also washed their bodies in the lake. I heard they were not allowed to come to our settlement because, someone said, they were hungry for our women. If they were to see one they might grab her and...you know the rest.

All during that same summer, the DC-3 airplane landed on the land strip. From that time until today, all kinds of airplanes have landed on that land air strip.

Two or three years later, the DOT people came on a ship with building material, and we Inuit were hired to help them build houses. The dollar bills slid down into our pockets, and they were precious to handle. I heard that one Inuk wanted to buy a telescope for ten cents, and the manager,

PLATE 8

King got caught by the angry waters — PBS Cliff Palace Canoe

Sandy Lunan, kicked him out of the store. Telescopes cost $30 to $50 each. Some Inuit used to think the metal money was worth more than the paper.

A little later the nursing station was built and a few government houses. One of the Army houses that was built across from the settlement was brought to this side and made into a school. We were glad to see all these things when they came. In those years, we began to see white women for the first time. I remember only a few before then. I have heard a story that the Inuit long ago used to think that the *qablunaat* were all men, no women. But at that time we began to see that a *qablunaat* could be a woman too.

All that time when buildings were being built and more *qablunaat* were coming to the Baker Lake settlement we didn't know they were taking over the settlement ground from us. We found that out when some Inuit put up their tent and were asked to move to another spot by a white man, because he said they might build another building soon and that they didn't want that spot to get dirty with garbage and other things. The Inuit usually just agreed and moved their tents away, even though they might not be too happy inside. So at the beginning, that is how the Inuit felt when outsiders started to move into Baker Lake. They were told what to do and what not to do, and they obeyed the commands. I think I should mention that there were commands given to all Inuit around Baker Lake before this time by the Anglican minister and the Hudson's Bay Company manager and the Police. Commands by those people were understood by Inuit. The Anglican minister could tell the Inuit what to do

and what not to do because it was in the Bible. Inuit believed the Bible with all their hearts. Even though they couldn't always live up to it. Commands by the Hudson's Bay Company manager were good for a hunter. He was not to stay in the settlement too long doing nothing, the manager used to tell him, he must get off to the land and hunt caribou and foxes. Even though sometimes the Hudson's Bay Company manager was quite hard on the Inuit they liked him very much. The Police commands were hard to understand but they were dangerous to disobey, so the Inuit did their best to obey them. That is, when they could not hide from them. The Inuk did disobey the policeman when he was out of sight. It was not hard to understand why—he didn't really know why he must not do this or that. But the white man, who does know, also disobeys the law, in the North that is, and we know that. Someone said to me one time, "Human beings sometimes become like animals when they are out of sight." This means that when a man or a woman is all alone, with no-one to see him, he will do anything.

By the end of the 1950s the settlement of Baker Lake covered most of the present site and the ground had been scraped with tractors. We used to complain a lot that where there were growing things scraped off it was like a person skinned. Where the houses are now, the ground has no skin anymore. It's all dead ground, no longer smelling of growing things. Instead there's a smell of stones, a dead smell.

Soon after that year, quite a few Inuit starved to death around the Back River area; I think there were about 24

PLATE 9

who died. From then on the government started to move Inuit into the settlement. I guess they thought the animals were getting scarce. But it was not because the animals were scarce; it was because most Inuit around Back River had no ammunition and no fish nets. At Ennadai Lake too the Inuit were often hungry during the winter. They told me they had no ammunition or fish nets. If they had them, they would have had all the meat they could use during the winter and wouldn't have had to come to the settlement to live on relief as they're doing now. When the government moved all the Inuit into settlements I don't think the Inuit knew they were going to stay in there for a lifetime. I think they still believed that some day they would be put back where they were before. Now they know that their dreams will not come true. There is no hope of going back to the land.

For some Inuit there is no time to think anymore in settlements, because there are things going on every day and every night; movies, dances, garbage to be collected, toilets to empty, the floor to be swept, dishes to be washed, clothes to look after. We must go to church, go to the Bay store and the government office. There are meetings of different kinds in different places about different things, record players booming inside the houses and even outside in some places.

But when you ask an Inuk about the old days compared with today, how he felt about the past and life today in the settlement, he says life is much easier today than in the past. And yet he is not happy; he doesn't know why. He's still looking back to the old days and wishes he had the chance to go back to the land.

When I drew this (PLATE 1) I was thinking of the dead ones and how my people used to think about them. Sometimes a dying Inuk would ask his fellow Inuit not to bury him with rocks on top of him when he died so that he would be free to help anyone that needed help. That is what some dying men said.

What about the living ones? What do they think about the dead? Before we became Christians I never heard an Inuk say that he would see a dead man again after death. Of course, we believe in an afterlife now after the missionaries taught us that from the Bible. But Inuit still somehow believe that the person's spirit is around after the person is dead. An Inuk believes that when you name your child after the dead one, then the dead one lives again in the name, and the spirit of the dead one has a body again. Until the name has been given the spirit is without a body. Another belief was that a dead man's spirit went to live in an animal until someone gave the name to an Inuk. When an *angakkuq*, a shaman, died, if this *angakkuq* had a helper while he was living, perhaps a wolf, then his spirit would go to live in the wolf. If his power was a caribou, then his spirit went to live in the caribou, or if his power was a dog, his spirit lived in the dog.

But more often, the dead ones are believed to be living in the Inuit who have their names put upon them. A woman who was pregnant would have a dream in her sleep about a person who died. To her it meant that the dead one wanted to be named in her baby, and she did give the name to the child when the baby was born. Then someone shouted,

PLATE 10

"inuuliriuuq," meaning "he lives again." Sometimes a person who was dying would ask the Inuit not to use his name for a woman, because he said he didn't want to be a woman. If his wish was disobeyed, they believed that the baby would die. And it seemed to work that way many times.

Let me tell about something I did against a dead man's wish. An old man died. When somebody died we dug a shallow hole in the ground and we buried him. But I was told that this old man didn't want to be buried under the ground, but wanted to be right on the top, without rocks over him. Being in the settlement we couldn't do that, and I told the Inuit so. And they agreed to dig a hole and bury the old man under the ground like all the rest. So we did that and we all went home.

At that time there was someone with me who was in missionary training for the Anglican Church. When we buried the dead the weather was just fine, no clouds anywhere to be seen and it was spring. The missionary and I were cleaning outside our house when suddenly a strong wind hit us, and all the cans and papers that we were gathering to be burned were lifted up by the wind and flying all around us. And when we looked about there were papers and garbage flying in the air. Clouds came over and covered us all and then rain poured down upon us, and this missionary said, "Is it really true, that something is happening?" I said, "It seems so, doesn't it?" Before that time we were told that if we disobeyed the old man's wish, there would be something unusual happen, perhaps even all the Inuit would die out. So the missionary and I went inside the house be-

cause we couldn't work anymore on account of the bad weather. I looked out the window, no Inuk to be seen anywhere. Then I heard a door open and shut in the other room. I went to look. Two old ladies were standing there, water dripping from their clothes down to the floor, holding in their arms some kind of a canvas. I said, "Suna?" meaning "What is it?" One said, "We want permission from you to go to the old man's grave. We would cover him with this canvas. It's raining and he might get wet. The rain might get worse and worse. If we cover him with this the rain might stop." I said, "Go." They went off. It was about a quarter of a mile away. The missionary and I were watching the weather very closely. A few minutes later the rain stopped. The sun came out again from the clouds and smiled on us again. "Is it really so?" I wondered. One thing was still in my mind. Since we had disobeyed the old man's wish not to be buried under the ground, were the Inuit going to die out? Including me and the missionary? Well, it hasn't happened yet, thank God.

The next morning quite early I went to the old man's grave, just to see what the two old ladies had done. Yes, they had put a blanket-size canvas over the grave, and put four stones on the four corners to hold the canvas down. Then I wondered what could be under that canvas. Anything? Or nothing? So I lifted one corner and looked under. I saw a cigarette pack and a box of matches. I reached out and took them. I opened the cigarette pack, three cigarettes in it, and then I opened the matches. There were more matches than cigarettes in the box. I threw them out as far as I could, and

PLATE II

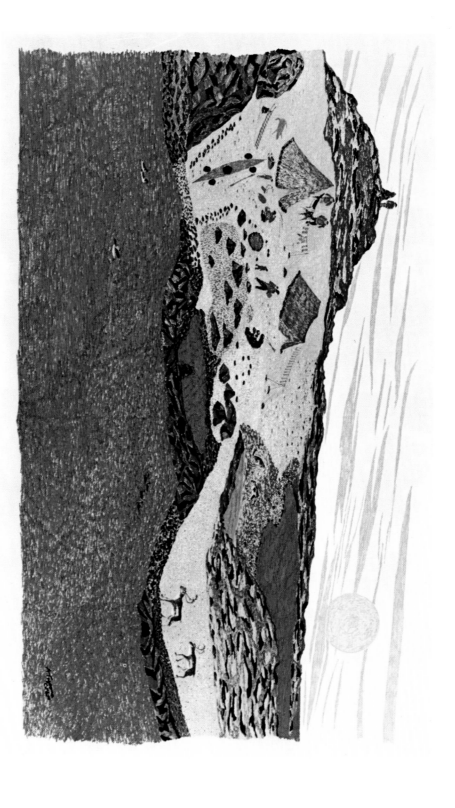

I took the canvas off and threw it away also. And there, standing, I prayed to God in whom I believed and trusted. I said, "Let not these things happen that seem to be happening, and let not the Inuit die out like the old man said. Let the Inuit live and not die to fulfill the old man's wish." I prayed these things because I believed that there are powers coming from both sides, good and bad. After that I went home, feeling better inside me.

This is a story I heard from the Inuit. The *angakkuq* was telling the others that when he died he would become a wolf because his name was Amaruq, meaning wolf. One day he got sick and died. His relatives buried him, with rocks of course. When the relatives were starting to walk back to their home and had walked about a hundred yards, his wife looked aback. Sure enough, she saw a wolf walking away from the fresh grave.

Here is another story, about another man who made a wish that when he died the Inuit should not bury him, just lay his body on the ground. He also made a wish that instead of mourning for him the Inuit should laugh when he died and afterward whenever an Inuk would go to see him lying on the ground there should also be laughter. One day this man got sick and died. The Inuit laid his body on the ground without clothes on. That is the way he wanted it. So all his front could be seen. When they laid his body to rest some of the Inuit wanted to cry and mourn as usual, but some others started to laugh, and soon all the Inuit around his body were laughing. But to them it was not right to laugh.

About a year later, one of the Inuit told the story of what

had happened. An Inuk who heard the story said that he could never have laughed at a dead man because this would not be right. So the storyteller asked the Inuk to come along with him to visit the dead man. The two of them went there. The Inuk who had said he could never laugh at the dead man started to laugh. The body was lying on a high cliff; all around were steep cliffs falling straight down, toward the sea water. It was an island. The man was laughing so hard that he fell and started to roll toward the edge, still laughing, but the other man ran after him and grabbed him before he fell into the sea.

In the old days, even in my lifetime, whenever a person died, they buried the body with some of the belongings of that person laid on the side of the grave. They said that the belongings were still his or hers, and that no-one else should own them. This taboo wasn't believed by everyone, but those who believed it usually laid all kinds of things by the grave. After the white men came to the North, some Inuit got canoes and boats and rifles. Sometimes a brand new rifle was laid by the grave, or a brand new canoe, and no-one was supposed to take them. One time I was walking along the high hills on my caribou hunt when I found a grave that was quite new, and a rifle was lying beside it. I took it and looked at it. It was still good, a little rusty. So I decided to take it home and I did. In my hunting tent I cleaned it and oiled it and polished it. It was like new. After that I went home to the settlement. There I showed it to the Inuit, but nobody was interested and their faces seemed scared. I knew they still believed in the taboo. One day I showed it to a man who

PLATE 12

told me to take it back where I found it. If the dead man's relatives heard what I had done, he said, they would be very unhappy. So I agreed. And I went back by canoe to the grave. I just put it on the shore of a lake; I didn't put it right where it had been. Somehow it bothers me a little every time I remember that rifle because I didn't put it where it was before. That wasn't really honest, the way I did it.

In this drawing (PLATE 2) there's the same idea as in the first one, the one with the skeleton: what happens to the spirits of the dead. The ghostly human forms seem to be in sorrow; they even mourn for something down on the earth in the graves. We have a belief that not all the dead are happy after death. Some are in sorrow while others are happy. In the olden days they believed that if a man murdered someone, the murdered man will live on in the man who killed him. The Inuit used to say that a murderer has a person in him, the person that he killed is in his murderer, unless before the murderer dies he confesses what he has done. They called this confession *amitat*, meaning bring out, or sometimes *miriaq* meaning vomit. Nearly all Inuit in the olden days, just before they died, confessed everything they could remember that made them sick inside. Some still do this.

Do the dead ever show themselves to the living? I am going to tell you now something that my own wife saw. I know you are going to say "imagination" or "seeing things that are not there." You may be right, and yet you could be wrong.

I know my wife. I have been living with her for 31 years. Am I saying that she has never told a lie? Well, she may have told a lie, like you and me, about something unimportant. But I can't help believing my wife when she is telling me something serious. And she saw her own mother with her own eyes after her mother had been dead for a few days. Can you believe that? Of course not. Do I? Yes I do.

My wife's mother was sick for a long time before she died in 1938. In those days no-one used to go to the hospitals down south and there was no hospital then in Baker Lake. The missionary tried to do his best to help her, but instead of getting better, she got weaker and weaker. When she finally died, there was nothing left of her body but skin and bones.

My wife, Auga'naaq, was thirteen or fourteen when her mother died. She used to go to the missionary's house with the other children for lessons three afternoons a week. After school she was walking toward her home, an iglu, when she saw her mother ahead of her, about 30 steps away. She thought, "Mother." At that moment she didn't remember her mother had died. She walked toward her mother, who was walking toward her. Then my wife looked away for a second to see where she was walking and when she looked up again, her mother had gone. While my wife could see her mother, she could hear her coughing too, as she always did. Then my wife ran home, not because she was afraid, but to tell her father. As soon as she went into the iglu she said, "*Anaanaga takulauqpara...*" that is "I saw my mother..." Her father said quietly, "Yes, before your mother died, she

PLATE 13

said that after she died she would come back to see you for the last time."

"I promise you everything." I think every man when he gets married feels this way (PLATE 3). Everything around him belongs to him and he wants to share it all with the woman he marries. When a man is getting married he feels himself rich because the world around him is given to him if he can just find a way of getting it. So he promises it all to his new wife. When a man is getting married he feels like a king. He feels there is no-one like him and no-one like his wife. They are the only two, the best of all; all the rest are ugly.

When I started to draw this picture (PLATE 4) I had no idea what to draw, so I started to rub the orange pencil without making an outline of anything. When it became larger and larger it seemed to me like a part of a human body. So that's the way this drawing came about. There's no story to it. It only makes you wonder what is going on. I know what you're thinking, Adam and Eve, love. Love wants to touch. Love wants to come to go right in if possible. Love wants to see very, very close, the closest possible. Love has no eyes to see which one to love. Because love is love, it loves all.

I have known a few women who ran away from their husbands (PLATE 5). This is still going on today but there's no danger anymore like there used to be in the olden days. Today women who aren't happy in their homes have places to go—the police or the missions. And if a woman runs away, many people will look for her and try to find her. But in the olden days, when a woman ran away in the winter, there were no camps she could reach before she froze to death. Yes, some did reach another camp if there were camps close enough. It was easier in spring or summer. But sometimes a woman ran away from a cruel husband to die, to freeze to death or jump into a river or lake. I remember one woman came into our house who had run away from her husband. She had walked about 50 miles—it was early spring. At that time I was too young to understand what was going on. I remember though, my mother welcomed this woman to our house and fed her and gave her some clothes. I heard of another woman who also ran away from her husband and she was never found. Another was found dead, floating at the edge of the lake. She was wounded by a bullet that was found in her body. The husband said that she ran away and never came back. The thing is, she didn't have a rifle with her. How could she have shot herself?

Some women had a most unhappy life in the olden days. When a husband was cruel, he could do what he liked with his wife, before the missionaries and police came to the North. A woman is too weak to protect herself and a cruel husband is too strong. But today, even if the husband is cruel, he can't do what he likes with his wife, because the police are there. There are still some Inuit who are cruel inside, but they cannot show it because these *pukiqtaliit*, or "yellow-stripes," are standing by.

PLATE 14

A man named Kiviuq was a famous hero in the old days (PLATE 6). There is a story that he married a goose. When the season was come for all the geese to fly South, she flew away to the south with all the rest of the geese, not because she didn't like Kiviuq, but because she must go South, as she always had, in the middle of the summer. So Kiviuq lost his wife and he decided to look for her by walking southward. After many, many days' walking he saw a big Inuk ahead of him. When he got closer to the big Inuk he noticed that he could see a hole through him, and through that hole he could see the land and water behind him. When he was very close by, the big Inuk turned quickly to him and said, "Where did you come from, behind me or from my side?" Kiviuq understood that this big Inuk would hate anyone who came to him from behind, because of the hole in him. So Kiviuq answered, "I came from your side." Then Kiviuq walked on and stood beside the big Inuk. He was making fishes out of wood, small ones and big ones, on the edge of the river. When this big Inuk finished the shape of the fish-like image with his sharp knife, he put some oily semen from his *usuk*, or penis, on them and threw them into the river. As soon as the fish-image touched the water it swam away, alive. Kiviuq wanted to cross the river so he could go on searching for his goose wife, and he asked the big Inuk to make a fish that was big enough to carry him across. And the big Inuk made one. Kiviuq sat on the big fish and the big fish carried him across to the other side of the river. And then Kiviuq went on looking for his goose wife. Many, many moons afterward, he found his wife.

One day Kiviuq, on one of his walks, saw a fox without clothes (PLATE 7). The fox had taken off her clothes and laid them on a rock to dry, and then the fox went into a hole in the ground. Quickly Kiviuq ran and grabbed the skin of the fox and went back to where he was hiding. In a short time the fox came out and went to the spot where she had placed her clothes, her skin. In terror she yelled, "*Nauk amira?*" that is to say, "Where is my skin?" Kiviuq stood up and said, "*Tagva*"—"here." The fox said, "I want my skin." Kiviuq replied, "You will have your skin back if you agree to be my wife." To this the fox said, "Yes, I agree to be your wife." Then Kiviuq walked to the fox and held her hand and gave her back her skin. And she became Kiviuq's wife.

A poor boy was living with his grandmother because his father and mother had died (PLATE 8). There were many boys and girls in his camp who despised him and did many cruel things to him. Even grown Inuit did the same. One day his grandmother thought of something the poor boy could do to teach them all a lesson. So the grandmother skinned a seal's head and put it over the boy's head. And she pushed the boy's head into a large water-holder to teach him to stay underwater without breathing for a long time. She repeated this every day until the boy could stay down for a long, long time, nearly as long as a real seal can stay underwater without breathing.

One morning, nearly all the Inuit were playing a game outside. It was a fine day, and sunny. The old grandmother said to the boy, "The time has come for you to go down

PLATE 15

under the sea water and swim out, but not too far. Then come up and show your seal head like a seal does, and keep doing this until all the Inuit men come after you in their kayaks to kill you. Listen carefully. When all the kayaks have gone out after you, you go under the water and then come up again so they can see you. When they see you they will go after you again. Then you can lead them toward the sea, to the middle of the sea water. When you have reached the middle of the sea water and the land is far behind and out of sight, and all the kayaks are still following, then put up your hands and feet above the water and shout, '*Anu-riiiiii*'—'The wind.' Repeat the same word three times, and then go down and swim as fast as you can back here and come to me."

The grandmother put the seal's skin over the boy's head, so the boy looked like a seal. The grandmother then went outside; after a little while she came back in and said to the poor boy, "*Atii*," meaning "Go." The boy went out and walked toward the sea water behind the camp. When he reached the water he went right in, and down he went to the bottom of the sea water, and swam toward the front of the camp where nearly all the Inuit were playing games outside their tents. When he got near the Inuit he came up, like a real seal. Nobody seemed to see him, so down he went and then came up again. This time someone shouted, "*Natsiq takannā*,"—"Seal, down there." The boy went down again. In a little while he came up again to breathe and to look about him. He saw that all the men were running to their tents and then down to their kayaks. The boy could hear them crying, "*Natsikuluk, natsikuluk*," that is, "Little seal, nice little seal." Kiviuq happened to be one of the men in the camp. In a little while all the kayaks were racing after the boy. The grandmother had told the boy to lead all the kayaks toward the middle of the sea water and he did just that. Out to nowhere he led them. The men in the kayaks shouted back and forth, "*Taka, taka!*"—"There it is, there it is." So the boy kept on and on until the land was out of sight. Then he went under the sea water and swam as fast as he could to get away from all the kayaks. At last he came up, put his hands and feet above the sea water and shouted, "*Anuriiii, anuriiii, anuriiii.*" Each time he said that word, he could feel the wind getting stronger and stronger. Before long the angry waters were roaring like a bear. Then he went under and swam back to the land and to his grandmother. Just before he went into their tent he looked out toward the sea. The water was white it was so rough. Big waves went up and down like a bear's mouth, swallowing the kayaks. Quickly he went in. His grandmother didn't seem to notice anything and didn't say anything. So the boy went to sleep. What about the men out in the middle of the sea water? Many were fighting the angry sea water, trying to paddle back to the mainland. But the land was out of sight. One kayak turned upside down; a man drowned, another one drowned, then another and another.

For days and nights those who were still alive tried to fight the water and the wind, but one by one all of them disappeared from sight before Kiviuq's eyes. Kiviuq was the only one still fighting the angry waters and the wind. When

PLATE 16

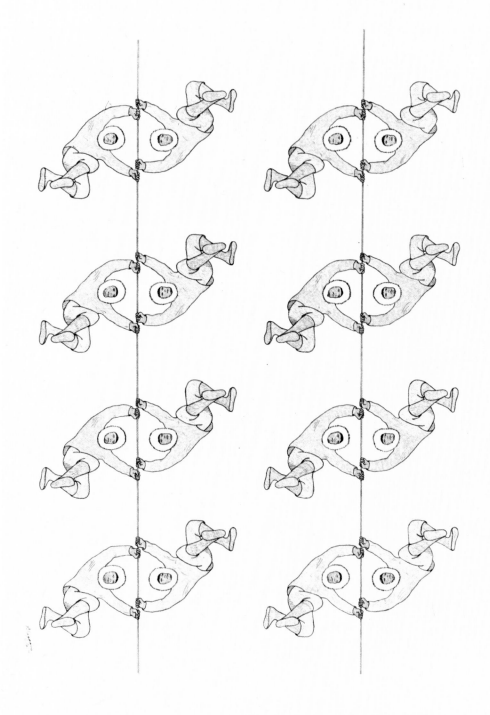

all the rest of the men were gone, the wind slowed down and the angry waters got quieter. Then a little sea bird came to Kiviuq and landed on the prow of his kayak and stayed there looking toward the land. The little bird seemed to be guiding Kiviuq. A few days later, Kiviuq saw land and said to himself and to the little bird, "*Nuna, nuna,*" that is, "The land, the land." The wind was still now and the angry waters no longer angry. There was a great calm. Kiviuq and the little bird reached the land, but not at his camp. They had come to the land where no-one lives. So a new life began for Kiviuq and for the little bird.

Sometimes men play a game, but in the back of their minds there is something more serious they really want to know, such as who is stronger or who is more outstanding. There is nothing wrong in this thought if there is no jealousy. But if there is, then the game can be dangerous. But these are not men in the drawing (PLATE 9). They are spirits, shadows. Shadows have a life of their own, their own games and tests of strength.

I would just love to get into this picture (PLATE 10). Wouldn't you? This kind of life was a wonderful and simple life. Everyone had something to do. I think that, instead of moving the Inuit into settlements, the government should have supplied them right in their camps. That way everyone could have been happy. If the Inuit must live together in larger groups than in the past, the government should have asked them to gather about a hundred in each camp, so help-

ing them and supplying them would be a little easier. The government should just help them, instead of feeding them all year round like they do now.

The Inuit used to go hungry part of the year; sometimes they starved, mostly because they never had enough ammunition for their rifles, or enough fish nets. Many of them don't even have canoes. So sometimes the Inuit go hungry even though there might be caribou around, or fish, just because they don't have what they need to catch them.

I still think that the olden days were the happiest days (PLATE 11) for the Inuit, so long as they had enough food all year round. The worst thing was the lack of food. They lacked food because they didn't have fish nets or canoes or rifles. Even when they had rifles they didn't have enough money to buy ammunition. And sickness came to them because they were hungry. They had clean air, clean water, new camping sites every year. The ground was clean. There was new fresh food every day when there were animals around and when they had enough ammunition or had fish nets and a canoe. But when the government decided to move all the Inuit into settlements I think they made a mistake. They should have given them what they needed in their own camps. If they wanted to teach the children, well, why not send a teacher to the camp? But now, this is too late. The government has to feed the whole family just because they want the children to go to school. I'm sure the government doesn't really want all the grownup Inuit to live in settlements. Why should they?

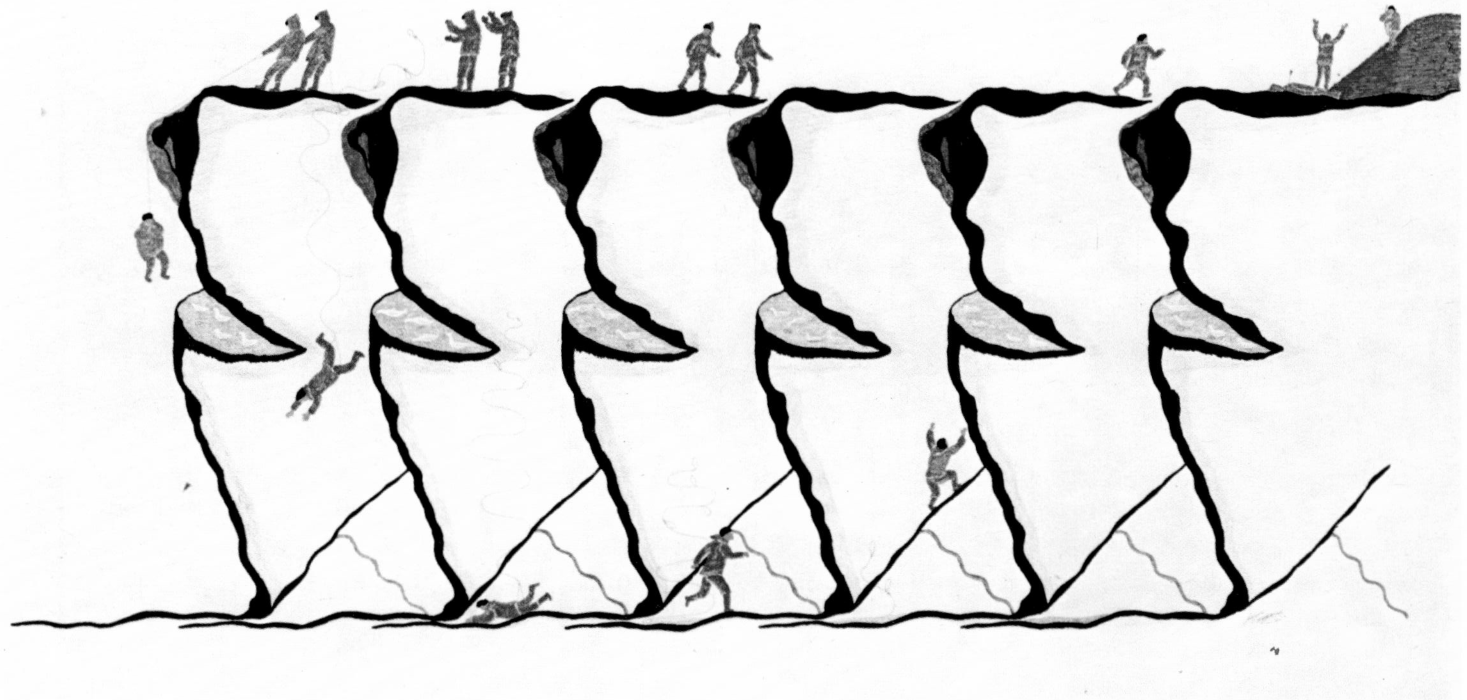

PLATE 17

I would just love to be in this summer camp, wouldn't you?

Drum dancing (PLATE 12) in the olden days was not just drum dancing. It always had something to do with spirits. Oh yes, during the dance the dancer did it for fun and sang his own song or sang with others. But by doing this he was telling others through the song things he could not tell them just by talking. As long as he's moving around and hitting the drum and dancing on the snow floor his shyness cannot be seen, and usually the singers closed their eyes too. Most of the time, the dance took place because the *angakkuq* was going to do something for the good of the camp and for the Inuit in that camp. Maybe someone saw a strange thing. The strange thing had to be killed or driven away from the camp. When the *angakkuq* was dancing, just before he went out to fight the strange thing, he would usually become wild. His face would change, his actions become strange, his eyes strange, his voice would take on a strange sound. They say that when this happens it means the *angakkuq's* spirit helpers are near to help him when he fights the strange thing. So, after his dance the *angakkuq* would run out and a little while later come back in, his hands full of blood. That meant he had killed the strange thing. Sometimes during the drum dance, if there was a strange thing to fight, all the lights were put out and everybody in the house closed their eyes. When the lights were out the *angakkuq* was supposed to fly out of the house and go down under the earth to fight the strange thing. They say the Inuit could hear the fighting under the iglu floor. When they heard the *angakkuq* come back into the iglu they put all the lights on again. Then the Inuit could see the *angakkuq's* hands dripping with the blood of the strange thing, and they all rejoiced that the strange and dangerous thing was dead.

This is just a happy drum dance (PLATE 13). It had nothing to do with spirits. The singers sang the song that was made by the dancer; it goes something like this:

Iyayiya ayaaya ayaayaaya, I am sitting in my iglu all the time,

Iyayiya ayaaya ayaayaaya, While another Inuk is out hunting *tuktu,*

Iyayiya ayaaya ayaayaaya, Even though I am doing nothing but sitting,

Iyayiya ayaaya ayaayaaya, One day I did bring that big *tuktu* down to earth.

Iyayiya ayaaya ayaayaaaaa.

Many times when you talk to an old man, when it is obvious what fate has in store for him, he often talks of when he was young, what he did and how he did it, and he also talks about the land where he used to live. When I drew this picture (PLATE 14) that is what I was thinking of.

There is a story that goes something like this: a woman was cleaning a fish on the edge of a big lake while her husband was standing by (PLATE 15). Suddenly a big fish appeared right in front of the woman and swallowed her.

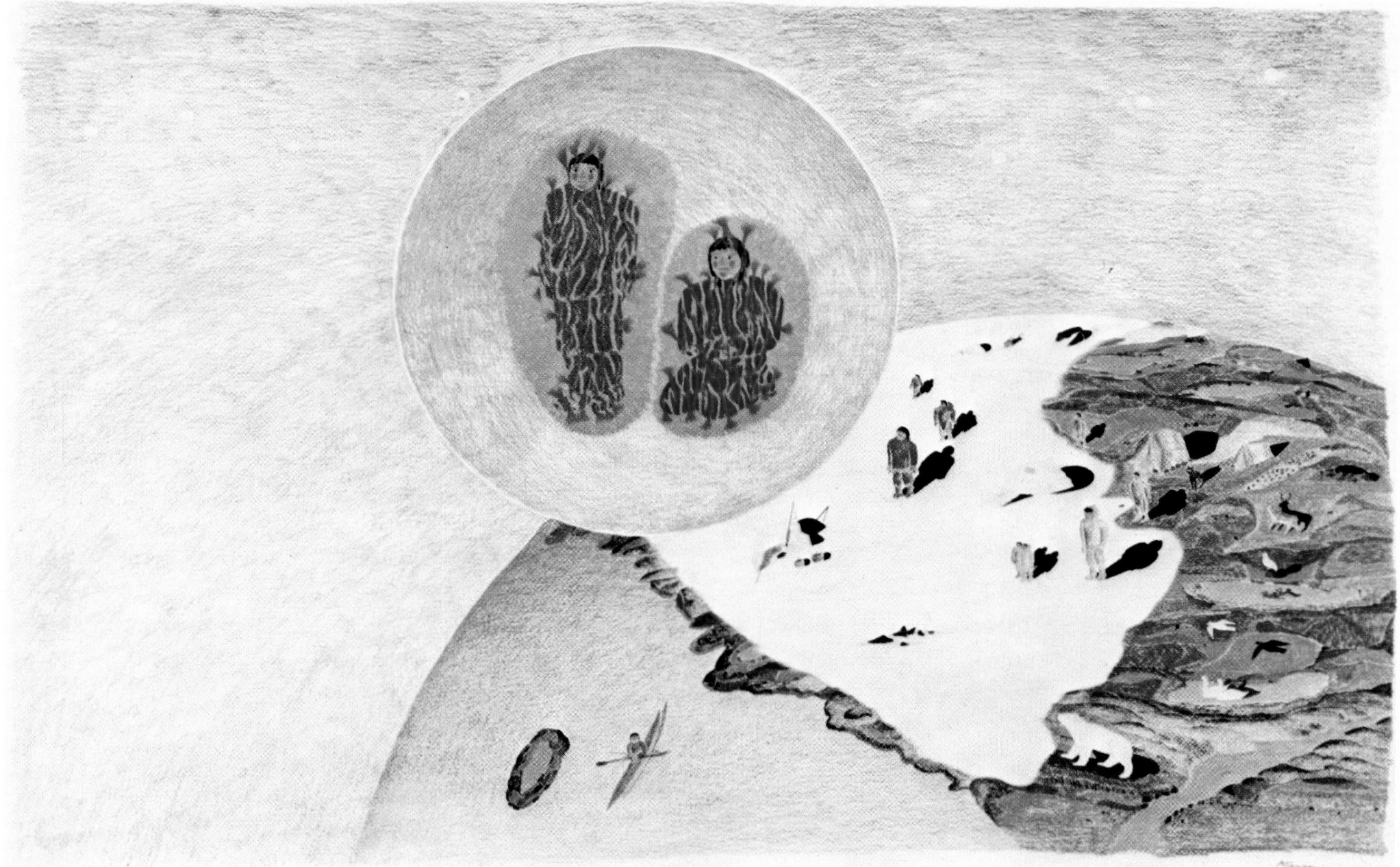

PLATE 18

The husband saw it all but could do nothing. It was too quick. So he thought of something that he might do. He grabbed his little knife and stood where his wife had been, hoping that the big fish might come back and swallow him as well. Sure enough, the big fish did come and swallow him. The man slid in and down into the stomach of the big fish, and he felt his wife. Then he started to cut the belly of the big fish until he felt water coming in. As fast as he could he cut a hole large enough for himself and his wife and grabbed his wife by her clothes and shoved her out and then himself out. He swam to the shore, and won the victory over the big fish.

This story is supposed to have happened at Dubawnt Lake, about 150 miles southwest of Baker Lake. Dubawnt Lake is bigger than Baker Lake. The Inuit are afraid of that lake, because, they say, it has big fishes, fishes that swallow human beings and even whole caribou. When I told the *qablunaat* the story they just laughed and said, "There is no fish that big that could swallow men. But there could be something else, not fish." Is there anybody who would like to go and see if there's any big fishes in Dubawnt Lake? There are stories too about the Inuit who used to make their camps and live around Dubawnt Lake. The Inuit call it Tulimaal-ugyuaq, that is, the place where there are big ribs. I think it would be interesting to take a look around Tulimaalugyuaq.

Very many years ago there was a poor man who lived with his wife among Inuit who were not so poor as they were (PLATE 16). The other Inuit could hunt and kill ani-mals, but this man could not hunt because he was weak in body. He and his wife lived with the help of the other Inuit who gave them the heads of their kill; nothing but heads was given to them.

One day the poor man's poor wife gave birth to a son. They named him, Atanaaryuaq. Part of the name, *yuaq*, means great or famous.

A year later another boy was born to them. They named him, Aamaryuaq. He too had *yuaq* for part of his name. The Inuit in the camp laughed at the poor man and the poor woman because they had two boys while they were being supported by the other Inuit. They said, "Poor man and poor woman make Inuit? How are they going to feed them?" Every time someone killed a seal or other animal the head was given to them for food.

When the two boys got old enough to lift the head of a seal, the hunters started taking them out to hunt with them, as helpers. Because they said, "If we are going to feed you and your father and mother, you must help us." So the poor man and the poor woman could do nothing to stop them from taking their two boys out to hunt. The two boys grew fast and were getting strong by doing all the work. Up to this time, the poor man and his poor wife and the two boys, Atanaaryuaq and Aamaryuaq, had eaten nothing but heads and sometimes something that was left over when the Inuit had been feasting together.

When there was a kill, the men all cached their meat for the future, while the poor man cached the leftovers and the heads.

PLATE 19

Sometimes the two boys played games with each other, because none of the other boys wanted to play with them. When they played together, the Inuit who watched them were amazed, because the two boys were throwing each other way up high and catching each other when they fell. They were also lifting very heavy things when they were out of sight of the others. They could lift a stone bigger than themselves. The Inuit didn't know that, even their poor father and mother didn't know. When the two boys played with heavy stones, they found they were very, very strong. Atanaaryuaq suddenly said, "Sangiyummarialuuyuguk" — "We are very strong." They also found that they could run very fast. Aamaryuaq said to his older brother, "We must tell no-one that we are the strongest men in the camp until we need to."

The two brothers grew very fast and soon they had their own dog team. One day all the men of the camp went with their dog teams to get some meat from their caches. The two brothers went with them to get some cached heads. After they had been to their caches, on the way home, all the dog teams started racing, trying to get home first. The two boys were riding their own dog team with a man riding with them. On the way home, when they were going very fast, the man pushed Atanaaryuaq off the sled, and then pushed Aamaryuaq off too. When Atanaaryuaq found himself off the sled and saw that his younger brother had also been pushed off, he knew this could mean death to both of them. It was too far to walk home. He shouted to his younger brother, "Taava," meaning "Go after him." The younger brother stood up and ran after their team. In no time he caught up with them and he threw the man off the sled. By that time his older brother had caught up to the team as well, so the two strong brothers rode home fast, leaving the man behind. The man was picked up by another team. After this all the men in the camp became jealous of the two boys because of what had happened.

The man who had tried to push the two boys off the sled went to the poor man's poor iglu and said to him roughly, "Your two sons tried to kill me by pushing me off the sled today and I would have died if there had been no other dog teams there. What do you say to that?"

The poor man said, "I'm sorry."

"Is that all you're going to say?" the man said.

The poor man said, "Yes." The man would have punched the poor man with his hands if he hadn't been scared of the two boys, who were watching him closely. So the Inuk left the poor man and went home. And the news of what had happened spread through the whole camp.

One morning all the men in the camp went out to hunt walrus. On the way out they met the two boys, who were going home even though it was early, dragging the whole body of a walrus. The Inuit were amazed because no-one had ever dragged the whole body of a walrus home before, without cutting the meat into small pieces first. Some of the men said to the boys, "Let us have a share of the meat." Atanaaryuaq, the older one said, "No, you will not."

One of the men said, "Why not? We have been feeding you two and your father and mother for years."

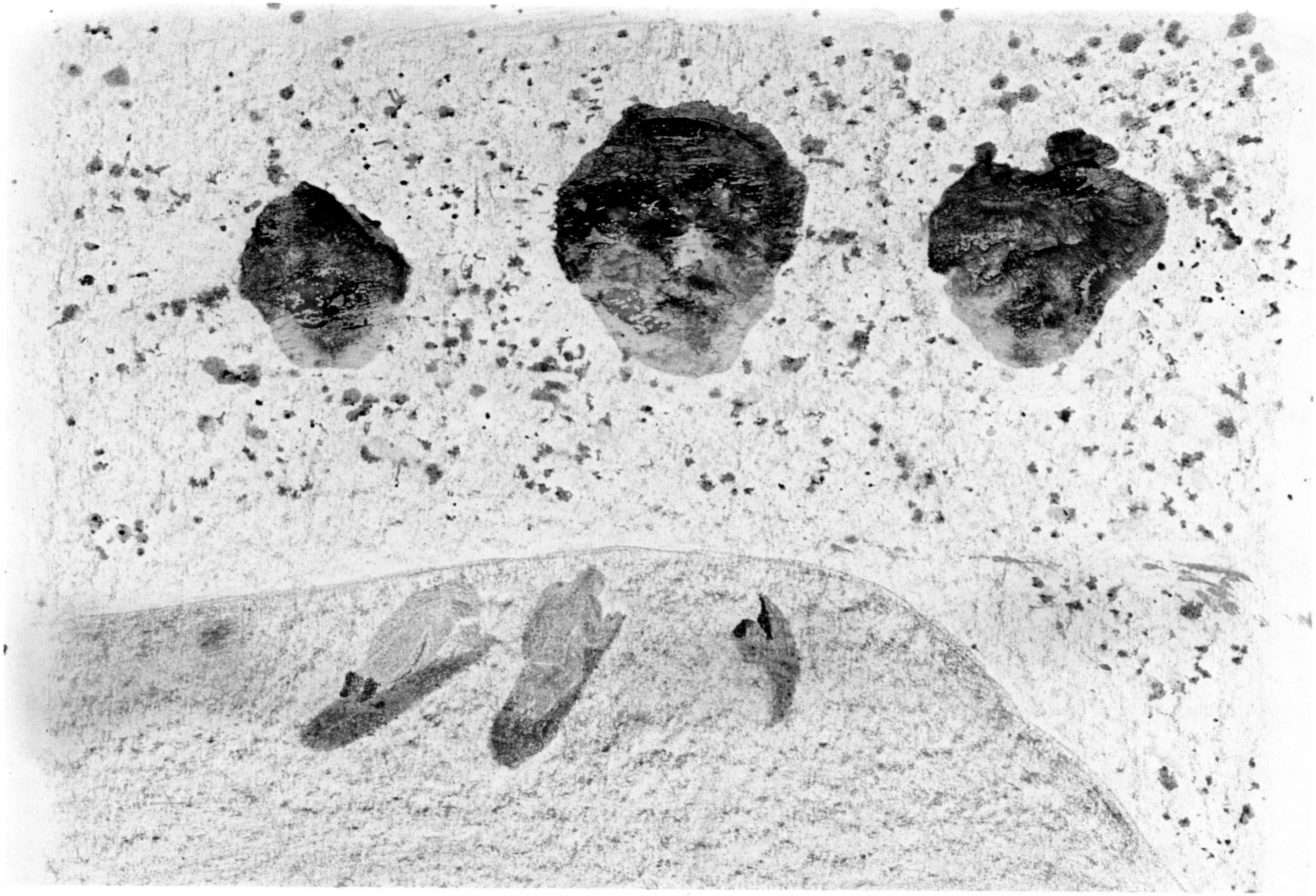

PLATE 20

The younger brother said, "Yes you have, but only with heads. This time our father and mother are going to have the whole meat for the first time. You will not have any share of the meat." The faces of the men were very angry, but no-one said anything or did anything. They feared the two boys now because of what had happened and because of what they could see for themselves: the two boys dragging home the whole body of a walrus.

From that time on the Inuit in the camp became more and more jealous of the two boys, by now two young men. Each had two wives. Because of this the Inuit hated the two more than ever, but they could do nothing.

Then one night in the summer, while the two brothers were asleep, the men surrounded their tent and went in and killed Atanaaryuaq, the older brother, with their knives, but the younger brother, Aamaryuaq, escaped and ran away. The Inuit ran after him. While Aamaryuaq was still running he found an old man and his wife who were living all alone. He told them what had happened. Then the old man hid Aamaryuaq by covering him with moss. When the Inuit arrived and asked the old man if he had seen Aamaryuaq, the old man said he hadn't. So the Inuit went back to their camp.

Later, Aamaryuaq married the old man's wife's daughter and went off to the inland. During the next summer he killed many caribou and had lots of meat for the winter. When the snow came he built an iglu. A large one, because he planned to invite the men who had killed his older brother to have a big meal in his iglu. He also made a whip with many tails, with pieces of bone at the end of the tails, and a pair of boots, with pieces of bone on the bottom so he wouldn't slip.

When everything was ready, he went out in the middle of the night to the Inuit camp, taking with him his best dog. When he arrived at the camp everybody was sleeping, so he looked into the houses to find his two wives. He saw one of his wives sleeping peacefully with a man. This wife he didn't love. He looked into another poor iglu. He saw his second wife crying because she was not cared for by the Inuit. This wife he dearly loved.

It was nearly morning, so he went off a little way and waited for the Inuit to get up from their sleep. In a little while one Inuk came out of his iglu and saw Aamaryuaq standing a little way off. The Inuk went in and soon more Inuk came out. All the Inuit in the camp came out with their bows and arrows. Aamaryuaq also had bow and arrows with him. At last one of the men in the camp shot an arrow at Aamaryuaq. Aamaryuaq's dog caught the arrow before it hit the ground and chewed it to pieces. Then arrows came flying at him from all the men of the camp. But Aamaryuaq kept moving, sideways and up and down, and his dog caught all the arrows and broke them to pieces. From time to time Aamaryuaq also shot an arrow at the men. Each time he killed one of the Inuk. When the men saw that they were losing more and more men they gave up and called Aamaryuaq to come in peace and he did. His wife, the one he didn't love, came out to meet him. Aamaryuaq took the hands of the woman and split them in half with his hands. The wo-

PLATE 21

man cried like laughing. Then his second wife came out. She wept in the arms of Aamaryuaq, and Aamaryuaq loved her. So Aamaryuaq took his wife, the one he dearly loved, and went back to his camp. But before he went back, he told all the men to come to his camp and have a big meal. All the men followed him. When they were nearly finished eating, he put on his boots that had bones on the bottom, and took his whip and jumped to the entrance of the iglu and started whipping them. And he killed them all; no-one escaped.

There were three men (PLATE 17) with their wives and children living together in the same camp. Two of the men hated the other man because of his wife. She was a good wife. They wished to have her.

One day in the springtime, when all the seagulls lay their eggs on the cliffs of the high hills, the three men decided to get some eggs for food. When they reached the top of the cliff, the two men who hated the third man asked him to go down the cliff on a rope while they held the other end. He could then collect some eggs in a bag. He agreed to go down. The two men tied the rope around him and let him down slowly. Suddenly one of the two men shouted "*Sapkunnialliqpaptigit*," meaning "We are going to let you go." The hanging man shouted back "*Uvatsiaru*," that is, "Just a minute." He quickly moved his body around, legs up, head down, facing the bottom of the cliff. When he had done that he shouted again, "*Atii*" —"Go ahead." The two men let the rope go. The third man, with the help of the long rope behind him, flew downward like a bird. When he landed he

was unhurt. Quickly he got up and ran to reach the camp around the hill before the other two men got there. When he reached the camp, the two men were not there yet. He got his bow and arrows ready. In a little while, the two men appeared, half running because they were so happy that one of them was going to have the dead man's wife as his wife. When the third man could see the two men's faces he went out from his tent and he let them see his face so they would know who he was. With his bow and arrows he killed both of them. He got for himself three wives and many children and lived very happily for a long time.

When I drew this I thought about the Inuk and his sister who went to the moon long before the white man went there (PLATE 18). There are stories about people who went to the moon in different times. But we don't know what happened to them when they got there. In the olden days we children used to be told not to look at the moon too long, because, they said, if you do, someone from the moon will come with his dog team and take you there. Or you will be hit by someone in the moon with an arrow.

The stars were all called names. Each star or group of stars had a different name, such as: Three men run after the bear. I don't remember all the rest but to us the stars were living things who were holding bright lights.

I drew the moon first with two people in it, the man and his sister, who are tied there so they cannot get loose and come back. When you look at the moon now you can see a man there, and a dog on his left side. The sister? She's be-

PLATE 22

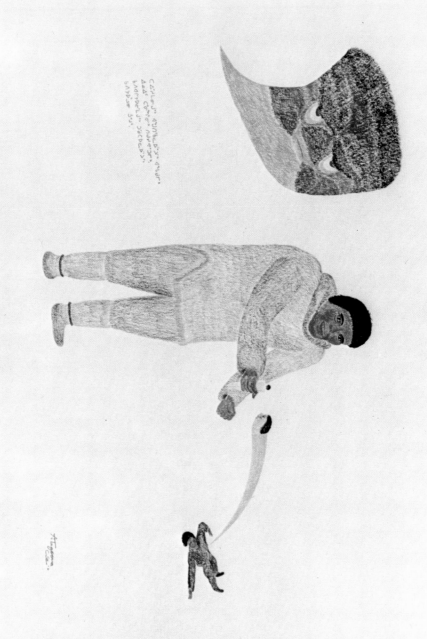

ground (PLATE 21).

In the time of my mother's mother, there was a powerful angakkuq (PLATE 22). Here is the story of how he became an angakkuq.

When he was a young man, he was quite content, living with his parents and his wife and children, with a few other families living around them. But when he reached middle age, he decided he wanted more power than he had over the other Inuit. He went to see one who was called angakkuq and said to him "Angakkuujumagamattauq," meaning "I want to be a shaman too."

The shaman told him to come the following evening. When he went the next night the angakkuq didn't seem to notice him, so he just sat down on the snow floor without saying anything. He sat there for a long time. Then the angakkuq said slowly, "I have built an iglu for you half a day's walk away from here. You go there tonight and stay there for five days. Do nothing day and night. Do not eat. Do not drink." He heard and understood everything the angakkuq said, but he sat waiting for more. He didn't say anything. After a long time the angakkuq said, "You heard me."

"Yes," he said, "yes, yes." Then he cleared his throat and said, "Now?"

The angakkuq said, "When I said 'tonight' I meant now."

The Inuk cleared his throat again and asked, "Where is the iglu you built for me?"

"Walk toward the moon, you cannot miss it." Then the

hind the face of the moon; you can't see her. What about the round world? Where did I get that idea? Did I ever see it for myself? No. Did you? Maybe if you ever go far enough you will see it all around. We must tell the Inuit not to look at the moon too long. But they can see that there is someone in the moon who was not there before. Even the animals notice something new in the moon.

When I drew this picture (PLATE 19) I was thinking of the Inuit who had died and left us. Where did they go? Well, hundreds, even thousands of times I have heard and read about heaven, where the souls of human beings go. They must be up there somewhere and they must still have their bodies because without a body there is no-one. If there is someone, he or she has to have a body, or timi. So, these are the souls of Inuit who we say tuquyut, or died.

There is no story in this picture (PLATE 20). You must make one for yourself out of that drawing. Are they not the Silaup inungit, that is, "people of the air"? Inuit used to believe that there is a silaup inua, or "Man of the air," who controls everything and watches the Inuit. When he comes in sight you must not stand on your feet or you might get hit on the head because your head might be a little too high.

The literal translation of "tarralikitaaq" or butterfly is "the quickly shadowing." When they fly very near the ground the butterflies can only be seen like shadows on the

PLATE 23

Inuk stood up and faced the doorway. The *angakkuq* said slowly, "Remember what I said. You must obey every word."

"Yes, of course," he said. Without looking back to the *angakkuq* he walked out into the empty night, toward the moon.

He walked and walked and walked. It was a cold night, but he was hot and sweating. The wind was behind him, pushing him toward the moon. After walking half the night he came to the iglu and went in. It was dark inside but he could see clearly. He could see that the iglu was very small; there was just enough room for him. And there was nothing at all inside it. He remembered the *angakkuq's* words, ". . . stay there for five days, do nothing day and night, neither eat nor drink."

The first night was hard enough to live through without eating or taking a drink of water after his long walk. Slowly the morning light shone into the iglu through the entrance, which was still open. Then he fell asleep. When he woke up the sun was down. He had slept all the first day. He needed a drink of water. But as soon as he thought about water he went outside to forget. He sat outside and looked at the moon. There was nothing else to look at. The moon seemed warm, though the land was cold.

The first day and night passed at last, and the sun was off the land toward the heavens.

Four days and nights passed and he didn't eat or drink. All he did was sit and sleep. And eat snow? No, not even that.

The fifth day began. Nothing had changed. There was nothing to see except the snow, the iglu, and at night the moon, stars and the deep heavens. Again he slept all through the daylight. In his sleep he saw something strange, something that lived and spoke. The thing looked like an animal and yet spoke like a human being. It seemed to appear from nowhere and come right out at him and say, "You will do what I say from now on and I will help you do whatever you ask. But remember, you should never, never forget me when you have important work to do, because I have someone else I must obey; when he gave me to you I became yours forever, or else you and I will die. . ." Then the Inuk woke up and thought of water.

"Water, water," he said loudly. But the words of the *angakkuq* came to him.

"Do not eat, do not drink. . . remember what I said. . . every word you must obey."

"Yes, of course," he thought. "I am getting weak, and this is the last night I must be here. Tomorrow morning I will go back to my home." Night came, the last night. He went outside and sat beside the iglu, looking toward the moon. When he had sat there a long time he noticed something under the moon, coming toward him. Countless needles struck his whole body, from head to foot. Then he thought, "Is that the thing I saw in my sleep?" When the thing came closer the whole land shook, and when it was closer still he knew what it was. It was a bear, a big bear, and yet it had a face like his own face. Then the bear said, "I will help you do whatever you ask or whatever you wish. . ." At that moment he fainted and did not wake up until morning came.

When he woke up the sun was already off the land. He started right away to walk back home. He didn't even think of water anymore; he was beyond that now. On the way home he met the bear that had his own face. The bear said "Remember, you are now an *angakkuq*. You now have power, but only through me. Without me you will ruin yourself." Then the bear disappeared. The new *angakkuq* went home. He had become a shaman. And he could feel new power in his body and in his speech.

Then the power that had come to the *angakkuq* began to control him instead of his controlling it. The Inuit in the camp were afraid of the power he had over them. He would hold in his hand the soul of a certain person. The man who had lost his soul, because the *angakkuq* stole it, would grow cold. If the *angakkuq* kept the soul too long the man might die from the lack of warmth. His blood would get too thick to go through his body. The *angakkuq* practiced this often to show his power to others. The Inuit got so scared of this *angakkuq* they decided to put him to death.

They voted one man to kill him. The *angakkuq*'s wife agreed to her husband's death because he was becoming more and more dangerous to the Inuit.

One day the Inuit knew that the *angakkuq* had gone out to fish through a hole in the ice. They had been watching him all the time. So the man who had been picked to kill him started walking toward the *angakkuq* from behind. In his hands he was holding an ice chisel with a long handle on it. That day was very windy and storming with snow. With

all the wind's sound the *angakkuq* could not hear the man's footsteps coming toward him from behind. When the executioner got very close to the shaman, he pushed the ice chisel right through his chest and pulled it back out. The *angakkuq* fell forward and died. At last the Inuit in that camp felt free to live again the kind of life they wanted to live, without fear.

Here is a true story that I heard from the old Eskimos (PLATE 23). I heard this same story from a few different storytellers. Each time it was told in a slightly different way, so I am going to try to put together all the different versions of the same story. I am not going to use the actual names of the Inuit. I am going to give them new names, which I hope will not be names of any Eskimos who are living now.

It happened during the 1800s. In that time there were whalers from the South who wintered in Hudson's Bay selling rifles, gun-powder, lead to make balls for bullets, tea, flour, cloth, wood to make sleighs, knives and so on. Some Inuit lived with these whalers and danced with them inside their big boat. These *qablunaat*, or white people, made something in a pot, or wooden barrel, left it for a while and then poured it into cups and drank some and gave some to the Inuit to taste. Some didn't like it, some did. Those who drank a few cups went crazy. This is not the story I wanted to tell; I bring this out because I want the reader to know that many of the Inuit already had a few tools and food from these whalers.

There were many little camps inland, and others along

the shore of Hudson Bay. Those who lived on the coast were called *tariungrmiut*, the Inuit who lived by the salt water. The Inuit who lived inland were called *asiangrmiut*, the Inuit who lived elsewhere. There were two particular inland camps about 90 miles apart that I want to talk about. Because something happened there that should not have happened. Some Inuit still remember the story told to them by an old woman who was there as a very young girl and whose mother was one of those murdered in one of the camps. I heard the story from that same old woman. She told it to my mother when I was about ten years old. I had forgotten most of it but I got the story again and again later from different storytellers. The old woman who was there died over ten years ago. Here is the story:

There was a man named Akaa, who sat between his two wives, Ulu and Teega, on the edge of their sleeping platform in his iglu, or snow house. His two wives were busy making new caribou clothing for their man. Akaa was smoking his stone pipe and sweating heavily because he was thinking very intensely about something. Then he reached over to the teapot and poured some into the cup and drank it and jumped to his feet onto the snow floor and stretched his arms and legs. "Ahhhhhhhhhhhhhh." Then he said to his wives quietly, "*Umingmaksiuriangrniarama*," that is, "I will go and look for muskox." At the same time he was wiping the sweat from his face with his rough, strong hands. It was night, very dark outside. There was another iglu in his camp. A man named Tunu lived there with his wife Iku and their two children. Akaa went out to that iglu and said to

Tunu, "Tomorrow I will go to look for muskox. Will you come?" Tunu agreed. Akaa went back to his iglu, picked up a knife and cut a big piece of meat from the caribou carcasses that were stacked on the edge of the snow floor. He ate it and drank some tea and smoked some more of his stone pipe. While doing this he walked back and forth on the little floor, sweating as he always did when he was thinking hard and planning something big.

He went outside to check the weather. He looked up to the sky and watched the stars to see if they were twinkling or not. This night they were not; it would be a good day tomorrow for travelling, he thought.

He went in again and jumped up to the sleeping platform between his two wives and took off his clothes and covered himself with caribou skins that were made into blankets, closed his eyes and tried to sleep. His wives were nearly finished with their sewing. Once in a while Akaa opened his eyes to check if they had finished. At last they put aside their sewing and drank some tea. The older wife Ulu smoked the stone pipe, took off her clothes and slipped between the skins beside Akaa. The younger wife, Teega, picked up the water bucket made from caribou skin, and went out to get some fresh water for the morning from the water hole that had been chiseled through six feet of ice. When she came back inside, she drank some more tea and took off her clothes and went to bed on the left of Akaa. The older wife lay on his right hand. Ulu was not yet asleep, and she dimmed the light of the stone lamp and lay down again to sleep. When the light was dimmed, Akaa opened his eyes and looked up to the air vent, the little hole near the centre of the ceiling of the iglu. Through it he could see stars, one by one, passing by and going out of his sight. He remembered his younger brother, Nuila, who, like the stars, had passed out of his sight last year when he took a wife and went to live with his father-in-law in another camp. "On the way to the muskox hunt I must see my younger brother," he thought. Again he was sweating. He turned around and picked up his stone pipe, filled it with more tobacco and smoked it, lying on his belly. Finally he put away his stone pipe and lay back again facing toward the younger wife.

When the morning came, everybody was involved in the work of getting things ready for Akaa's and Tunu's travel. The *qamutik*, sleigh, was all loaded with the things that were needed for the journey, and five dogs were harnessed and made ready to go. They shook hands first and the two men Akaa and Tunu moved out and left the camp. They travelled all day and camped when it got too dark to travel. On the sixth day Akaa and Tunu saw a dog team coming toward them. When they met it, they saw it was Akaa's younger brother, Nuila, all alone. Akaa was sweating again as he always did when he got excited. He noticed that his younger brother's face was sad, nearly crying. Akaa asked him, "*Suvit?*" "What is the matter with you?" Then Nuila said "My father-in-law took my wife away from me and gave her to another man, Naavaa." Akaa, sweating more than ever, said loudly "We're going there; you will come too. We will be there tonight. I want to talk to him and find out what kind of man he is." He added, "Why did he do

that?" Nuila said, "Because he said I am not a good hunter, while the other man to whom he gave his daughter is a good hunter." "*Iwaluk*" or "Yes-no-good," Akaa said with an angry sound. Then he started the dogs and moved on toward the camp, and Nuila turned around and went with his older brother. There were two teams now and three men, Akaa, Tunu and Nuila. The wind was getting a little stronger and snow was drifting on the ground. A clear sky, it was cold, the sun was getting low. The two teams were travelling against the wind.

They would soon be in sight of the camp. Akaa turned to the left toward a little hill. He wanted to come from behind it and not be seen by the camp Eskimos. When they reached the hill he ordered the dogs to stop. When his younger brother caught up to them he also stopped. The sun was nearly touching the edge of the flat earth. Akaa said to the two, "We wait here for the dark." Then Akaa got his rifle off the sleigh and gunpowder and lead balls, and said, "Come," and he walked toward the top of the little hill, which was very near. The two followed him. When they reached the top they could see two iglus, only a quarter of a mile away from them. The three men lay close to the ground so they could not be seen by the Inuit of the camp if one of them happened to go out from the iglus. There were only seven Inuit there, and no children. Tuulik, the man who took his daughter away from Nuila and gave her to another man, was the head man there. Naavaa, the other man, also lived there. The Inuit in this camp were:

Tuulik, the head man
Akuk, his wife
Naavaa, Tuulik's new son-in-law
Ana, his wife
Taava, another man in another iglu
Anauki, his wife
the old woman who could not walk, as her legs were half dead for many years

Akaa knew all these Inuit. The three men watching the camp from the hill waited for the dark night. While they watched, one Inuk came out from one of the iglus and ran to the next. When Akaa saw him he said, "Too bad, he doesn't know that this very night he is going to die." Then the other two men knew for sure what was in Akaa's mind, that he was planning to do something horrible. Akaa told the other two his plan. Tunu was horrified but neither said anything. The three men quietly waited. Dark night seemed very slow to come that night for Akaa, but the other two wished the dark night would never come. But it came. They could see the light through the ice windows, one on each of the two iglus. Just before the dark night hid the camp from their eyes, they noticed that all the men in that camp went into one iglu, while the women went into the other. Akaa knew what they were doing. They were having a big meal. This was the custom of the Inuit in the past, when someone caught fresh meat, caribou, fish or muskox.

Then Akaa said, "Let's go." His brother, Nuila, and the other man, Tunu, followed Akaa who walked quickly toward the camp. Nuila carried the rifle, gunpowder and the balls made out of lead. Akaa was sweating very heavily again. When they got near the camp he said, "I'll go in alone where the men are. You two wait in the porch. Have the rifle ready." When they reached the iglu they went in and the two men stopped in the porch, Nuila with the rifle in his hand, loaded and ready to fire.

Akaa, without stopping, went right inside the iglu and the men, who were surprised to see him, said, "Tikippiit?" meaning "Have you arrived?"

Akaa said, "Ii," that is "Yes." Akaa found the men, Tuulik, Taava and Naavaa, eating the cooked caribou heads.

Taava said to Akaa, "Nirigit," meaning "You eat."

Akaa said, "I'm not hungry." As he said this he sat down on the edge of the sleeping platform right beside Tuulik, who was still eating his meat. Akaa said to him, "Tuulik, did you take your daughter away from my younger brother?"

"Yes I did," Tuulik said.

Akaa then said, "Let me have back all the things we gave you when my younger brother took your daughter as his wife."

Tuulik answered him, "No, you will not."

There was a really fine dog inside the iglu. Akaa said, "Let me have this dog."

Tuulik said, "No, you will not have him."

Then Akaa said, "Let me have those piles of skins." There were muskox skins on the edge of the snow floor.

Tuulik answered, "No, you will not have them." Right

then Akaa jumped to where he saw an axe, and he grabbed it and swung and with it he hit Tuulik just under his neck and cut a big hole. Blood poured out but Tuulik did not die. While this was happening, Taava and Naavaa were trying to get out of the iglu, but Akaa's companions pushed them back by pointing a gun at them. Akaa went out to the porch and grabbed the gun and pointed it at the wounded man and fired. Tuulik dropped dead. At the same time one of the men in the iglu put out the lamp and nobody could see in the dark.

Akaa handed the gun to his younger brother and said, "Load it." When the gun was loaded, Akaa asked his brother to go to the next iglu and get a light, a lamp.

Nuila went to the iglu where the four women were and asked for a light. One woman said, "Why is the light out?" Nuila said, "Someone knocked it."

One of the women said, "What was that bang we heard?" Nuila said, "Oh they're cutting frozen caribou meat with an axe." While Nuila was getting a light, one of the women ran outside to see, because they were sure the sound was not made by an axe. Akaa and Tunu were standing outside the porch when the woman came out. It was only a few steps away but Akaa did not know that she was a woman. He pointed the gun at her and fired and she dropped to the ground and died. Soon after that Nuila came back to Akaa and Tunu with the lamp lighted again. Akaa told him to hold the lamp, take out the ice window and shine the light through the hole so he could see the two men inside the iglu. By this time the gun was loaded again and ready to fire.

Nuila took out the ice window and held the lamp in it to light the inside. Akaa went to the porch. Through the entrance of the iglu he saw one man, pointed the gun at him and fired. Naavaa was hit. In a little while he was dead. Akaa went out and again told his brother to load the gun. One more man was left inside the iglu. Nuila loaded the gun and again held the light to the hole to shine in, while Akaa waited in the entrance for the man to appear inside the iglu. But the man inside moved back and forth so quickly Akaa couldn't aim the gun at him. While this was going on, a woman came out from the other iglu and stood beside Nuila, near the hole, and was appalled at what she found.

The man inside the iglu shouted, "First let me see my wife."

The woman called to him, "He's killed your wife." That was the woman Akaa killed outside. Right then the man who was hiding gave himself up and Akaa fired the gun at him. The man, Taava, dropped dead. Akaa had killed four.

By this time the two women were standing outside, horrified and crying out, "*Suvit, suvit, suyatinukua?*" that is, "Why you, why you, why did you do it to them?"

Akaa didn't hear anything. The two women outside were Tuulik's wife, Akuk, and Ana, the woman Akaa was fighting for—his younger brother's wife. There was one more woman there, the old woman who couldn't walk. She was inside the iglu. It was still the middle of the night. Akaa had had enough killing. He had killed all the men in the camp, and one woman by mistake, because it was dark and he could not tell she was a woman. He was sorry he had killed her because he liked women. Why should he not have three wives, or four?

Then what? The three men, Akaa, Tunu and Nuila stood outside; the two women went inside the iglu where their husbands lay dead. Nuila could have his wife back, and Akaa could have Tuulik's wife, Akuk, as his own wife for the time being until they reached home. None for Tunu? Tunu was very quiet and a good man. Akaa decided to go and see the old woman who was inside the next iglu, very near by. He found her crying quietly. She knew what had been done; one of the women told her all about it. Then Akaa wondered why he had done these terrible things. He wanted to cry with the old woman. He thought, "What about the time past when we, they and I, used to have fun and games and hunts together? Now they're dead, I killed them, what is the matter with me?" And he put out his hands; he wanted to shake hands with the old woman. She refused. Akaa wiped off the tears and sweat with his rough, strong hands, looked around a little and went out to the two men, still standing where they were before. They were crying too, quietly because they could hear the two women weeping and crying inside the iglu where their husbands were dead. Akaa looked up to the sky as if for some answer. He could tell what the weather would be the next day. He told his companions to get the dog teams they had left just beyond the little hill. The two men walked away quickly, obeying his order. Akaa went into the iglu where the three men were dead and the two women still weeping. When Ana, the wife of his brother, saw Akaa come in, she walked out.

Akaa said to Akuk, who stayed in the iglu, "Get all the things you need and get them ready. I'm taking you to my camp as soon as the daylight appears." And after he said this he took her to himself as a wife. She had no choice. He had already killed four; he could kill again. So he raped her on the sleeping platform beside the two dead men, with the third corpse lying on the floor.

After that, Akaa went to see the old woman and told her she would come with them in the morning. She refused to go but Akaa said she would be forced to come. And he told the woman Ana that she too was coming with them. By that time it was nearly morning, and the daylight was just appearing from the east.

Tunu and Nuila arrived with the two sleighs and dogs. Akaa told them to get ready to leave, to get all the things the three women wanted and put them on the two sleighs with their own things. When everything was ready, Akaa went into the iglu where the three women were weeping together. He forced them to come with him to the two sleighs. He gave the order to the dogs to go and they left camp. It was still a little dark. The sun had not yet left the edge of the flat land, but they could see well now. In Akaa's sleigh were Akaa himself, Tunu and Akuk. In Nuila's sleigh were Nuila, Ana and the old woman. Akaa had ten dogs to pull the sleigh; five extra that had belonged to Tuulik. Nuila had seven dogs, three of his own and four that had belonged to Taava.

They travelled all day. Because of the heavily loaded

sleighs the two women walked ahead of the teams to encourage the dogs to pull harder and faster; Akuk ahead of Akaa's team, and Ana ahead of Nuila's.

They were travelling toward another camp two sleeps away. On the second day the teams were getting very slow, because of the heavy sleighs. The dogs were getting tired. More and more often Akaa looked at the old woman who could not walk. She was half sitting, half lying on top of Nuila's sleigh, which was much slower than his. Often he had to wait for Nuila to catch up. Then Akaa stopped his team. Nuila caught up and stopped just behind him. Akaa said to the old woman, "Get off the sleigh." He helped her as she tried to get off, though her legs were half dead, until she was on the snow. By this time Akuk came, and she and the old woman wept together. The old woman was her mother-in-law. They knew what Akaa was going to do. Akaa told Nuila to leave. Nuila gave the order for the dogs to go and the team left, leaving the old woman behind. Akuk stayed with her until Akaa called her to leave the old woman and come to him, or, he warned her, "I'll shoot you too." Akuk then ran to the sleigh, pulled out the *pana*, and ran back to give it to the old woman, saying "*Miuniriyanniaqputit*," or "You will be looked after."

"By whom? And how?" the old woman thought. "I cannot walk. I can only move on my knees." Akuk left her and started walking, following Nuila's team, which had started ahead. Akaa gave the order to his dogs to go. Slowly they moved out. The dogs kept looking back to the old woman and moved out. Akaa shouted to the dogs in anger

so they looked back no more. The day was calm, no wind, no little cold. It was the middle of the day when they left the old woman. Akaa and his companions travelled until late at night. When they stopped, they built a little iglu for each group of travellers; Akaa and Akuk in one iglu, in the other Nuila, Tunu and Ana. No more old woman with them. No doubt she was dead by now, frozen to death. "Oh well, she was old and could not walk," Akaa thought.

Morning came. The two groups loaded their sleighs and left again. Since they left the camp nobody had spoken. There was very little for them to eat and nothing for the dogs. Akaa was heading for another camp that night. After travelling all day they arrived at the camp after dark. Akaa knew this camp; he had been here before. And he knew Tuulik had very close relatives in the camp. In fact, Tuulik's younger brother, Tiku, lived here with his wife, Naulik, and their six-year-old son. There were three iglus, quite a distance apart. Akaa and the other team stopped very near to Tiku's iglu. Then Akaa told Nuila and Tunu to go and enter the iglu. He pulled out the gun, which was always loaded, took more powder and balls and followed the other two to the iglu of Tiku. It was a dark night but they could see because they had been outside for a long time. Their eyes were adjusted to the dark by now. Nuila and Tunu walked right in. Akaa stopped outside with his gun pointed to the entrance, hiding a little. The two women, Akuk and Ana, rested beside the sleighs on the snow ground quite a distance away. After awhile, Akaa heard someone coming out of the iglu. He got ready to fire the gun. Yes, Tiku was coming out slowly. He didn't have his hood on. Akaa recognized him and fired his gun at his head. The man was hit and nearly fell but managed to stay on his feet. Akaa had no time to reload the gun. Tiku turned around and saw Akaa and moved quickly to grab him. Akaa dropped the gun and grabbed Tiku. They fought, each trying to put the other man down. Tiku had been hit by a bullet on the side of his face. This made him weak, and Akaa forced him down. Akaa had a little knife hidden under his *atigi*, or inner parka; it hung from his neck. He reached in for it and shoved it in just above the man's hip. The man curled and became still. Akaa got up and loaded the gun with gunpowder and then a ball. He went into the iglu and right away fired at the woman, Tiku's wife, Naulik, who was kneeling on the sleeping platform. She fell backwards and died. The two men, Nuila and Tunu, rushed out and ran to their sleighs. To them it was too much now to watch human beings killed. Tiku was dead outside the iglu; his wife, Naulik, was dead inside. The little boy, six years old? The little boy, now alone with Akaa, was not even weeping or crying anymore. He was beyond that. And now what do you think Akaa was going to do with that innocent little boy? He reached out and grabbed the boy and carried him outside toward the open water. At that time of year, after the coldest months, the river ice, which was thin all year round, was cut open by the movement of the river. While Akaa walked he was heard saying, "Some day this boy would grow to be a man, and would fight back for his parents." When he reached the open water he threw the little boy in. As soon as he hit the water he was gone. The boy was the seventh that Akaa had killed. By this time nearly all the Inuit in the camp were standing outside, near their iglu entrances, terrified, but no-one was doing anything; just standing where they were. Why did no-one do anything? These Inuit knew that Akaa was killing himself by doing all this. The things you do to others, those things will come back to you, all of them. So they didn't have to murder the murderer—he would do it himself.

Akaa ordered the two men, Nuila and Tunu, to build iglus so they could rest. And they did. Or did they? No-one knows. When the morning came, there were some Inuit standing outside but no-one came to Akaa and his companions.

From this camp Akaa was planning to go right on to his own camp, about six sleeps away. When the two teams were ready, they left the camp and headed southward. On that day, after about half a day's travel they stopped at a lake for fishing. They chiseled through ice five to six feet thick, let down their fishing hook with a line, and caught enough fish for their dogs and themselves. Enough for a few days. They fed the dogs, which were very thin now, and Akaa and his companions ate fish and drank water before they left again to travel the rest of the day.

After four days' travel, Akaa must have been thinking very hard; he was sweating again. By the fifth day they were out of food; there was nothing to eat. As usual the two women, Akuk and Ana, were leading the teams by walking in front of the dogs. That day one of the dogs was left behind because of starvation—he could not walk anymore.

Somehow Akuk, who was leading Akaa's team, found out that Akaa was planning to kill her that day. She was an *angakkuq*, a person who has power beyond her own power. In dreams she knew things that were planned against herself or someone else. That day she noticed that the rifle was loaded and easy to take from the sleigh. She knew what was coming, and she said something to the air which Akaa could not understand. The words were strange ones, because they were from the unknown powers. After they stopped to rest, Akaa ordered Akuk to walk again ahead of his team. When Akuk turned around Akaa quickly grabbed the gun, but before he could point it at her, the gun fired in the air by itself. Akuk didn't even look back. Akaa put the rifle back as quickly as he had taken it. He could tell that his plan was known, because the trigger in the gun was pulled by an unknown invisible person fighting against him and protecting Akuk. Who could that be? Tuulik, the husband of Akuk whom he killed? Or could it be the little boy whom he threw into the open water? Or any one of the Inuit he killed. Seven souls were with him, the souls of the seven he had killed. When a person kills another person, the soul of the dead man never again departs from his killer until the killer himself dies. Akaa knew all this, and he was shaking and sweating; he was scared.

Akuk was quite a distance away by now. She kept walking without ever looking back. Akaa ordered the dogs to go, and he left. The other dog team followed.

The next day they arrived home. Akaa's two wives and

Tunu's wife and two children came out to meet them—happy at first. But they soon sensed something was wrong. After the things from the sleighs were put away and the dogs let loose from their harnesses, Akaa's two wives went into their iglu. Akaa followed them, and then Nuila and his wife, Ana. Tunu went to his own iglu with his wife, Iku, and their two children. Akaa went with them. Inside the iglu, Akuk started to weep and cry. Then Tunu's wife asked her husband what had happened. He told her everything. Then everyone in the iglu cried. In Akaa's iglu no-one said anything. Akaa's two wives got the food ready for them to eat. The tea was boiling. Akaa announced he had something to say before he ate anything. Sweating as usual, he said in a low voice, "I killed seven."

Then his two wives became happy and laughing and said, "*Alianait*," or "This is happy indeed." The two wives thought their man had killed seven muskox. Then Akaa told them what he had done in a clearer way, that he had killed seven human beings to get the wife of his younger brother back. And in this iglu too everyone, except Akaa, now wept and cried. He also told them about the old woman they had left behind, because she was too heavy to ride on the sleigh and too old for anything. (By the way, the old woman was found, still alive, by a hunter. Day by day she had crawled, moving a little each day. The snow knife was her only protection. With it she built a little shelter when she moved to new ground. She was very thin and her knees were worn out, but she was brought to the warm camp and survived, thanks to an unknown protector who had given her warm blood, very warm it must have been for her to keep warm until she was found.)

Akaa wondered many times about the old woman. He thought she was, no doubt, the eighth human being to die under his cruelty; he never knew she had survived. Before he could find out he was dead himself.

About ten days from the time Akaa and his companions arrived home, after the dogs were fed and fat, and everything seemed to be quieting down, and he himself had rested for long enough, he left the camp with his two wives to hunt the *umingmak*, the muskox. He didn't ask anybody this time to go with him. Just himself and his two wives, Ulu and Teega. He planned to go around the camp where he had killed human beings, because that place could be very dangerous for him. The souls of the dead might fight back when they saw their bodies dead. The souls were with him now, and he wanted to keep them far from their bodies.

Six or seven days after they left home, a very bad snowstorm overtook them from behind, that is from the south, and the wind, a strong wind drove them ahead. Although Akaa couldn't see very well in the storm, he kept travelling. He didn't know he was heading right into the camp where he had killed three human beings, and thrown the little boy into the open water. Before Akaa recognized anything, the dark night came, and he stopped to build an iglu for the night's rest. After everything was finished Akaa and two wives lay down to sleep. Right away something hit Akaa from the back, that is from underneath. Quickly he stood up and groaned. His wives got up and put their hands on

him to hold him up. Akaa fell backwards as he was hit again from the back. "Let me up, let me up," he shouted.

His two wives got him to sit up, very stiffly and with great difficulty and deep groans. In his pain, sounds came through his lips. With groaning sounds strange to all of them, Akaa fell backwards again and again. When his wives got hold of him and set him up, his back tightened as a rope tightens. He couldn't stay up and yet couldn't sit anymore. By this time he saw things his two wives couldn't see. He shouted, "The boy, the boy and all the rest are here and they are coming at me." The two wives knew now that the souls of those Akaa had killed were fighting back. Akaa knew that too. What he didn't know was that he was just a few steps away from the camp where he had killed Tiku, his wife Naulik and the little boy. So the souls came back to the three bodies, and were fighting their killer. And they were killing him now slowly. Akaa struggled for life all that night and those he had killed were around him, all the night long. They were all there: Tuulik, Anauki—the woman, Taava —Anauki's husband, Naavaa, Tiku, Naulik—wife of Tiku, and the little boy. But where was the old woman? She was not among those he had killed.

And so, Akaa confessed everything he could think of during this suffering and struggling for life, and then groaned a deep groan and breathed no more.

We acknowledge with thanks the generous assistance provided by the Social Development Division of the Department of Indian and Northern Affairs and the Ontario Arts Council. The colour transparencies were made and supplied by the National Film Board through Alma Houston of Canadian Arctic Producers. The publishers are grateful to her for her early help, to Graham Rowley for his contribution to the historical accuracy of the manuscript and to Inuit Tapirisat for advice on the standard orthography.

Printed in Canada

ISBN 0 88750 168 0

Cover photograph of Baker Lake by Gail Low. Book design by Michael Macklem.

PUBLISHED IN CANADA BY OBERON PRESS